TO BOOK THE FOOD INTELLIGENCE ONLINE PROGRAMME

To use this book successfully, we recommend that you purchase the Food Intelligence Online Course which is used in conjunction with this book. Please go to, admin@fullpotentialtraining.com.au to purchase the course. Both the book and online course are ideal for School, Group and Holiday Programmes.

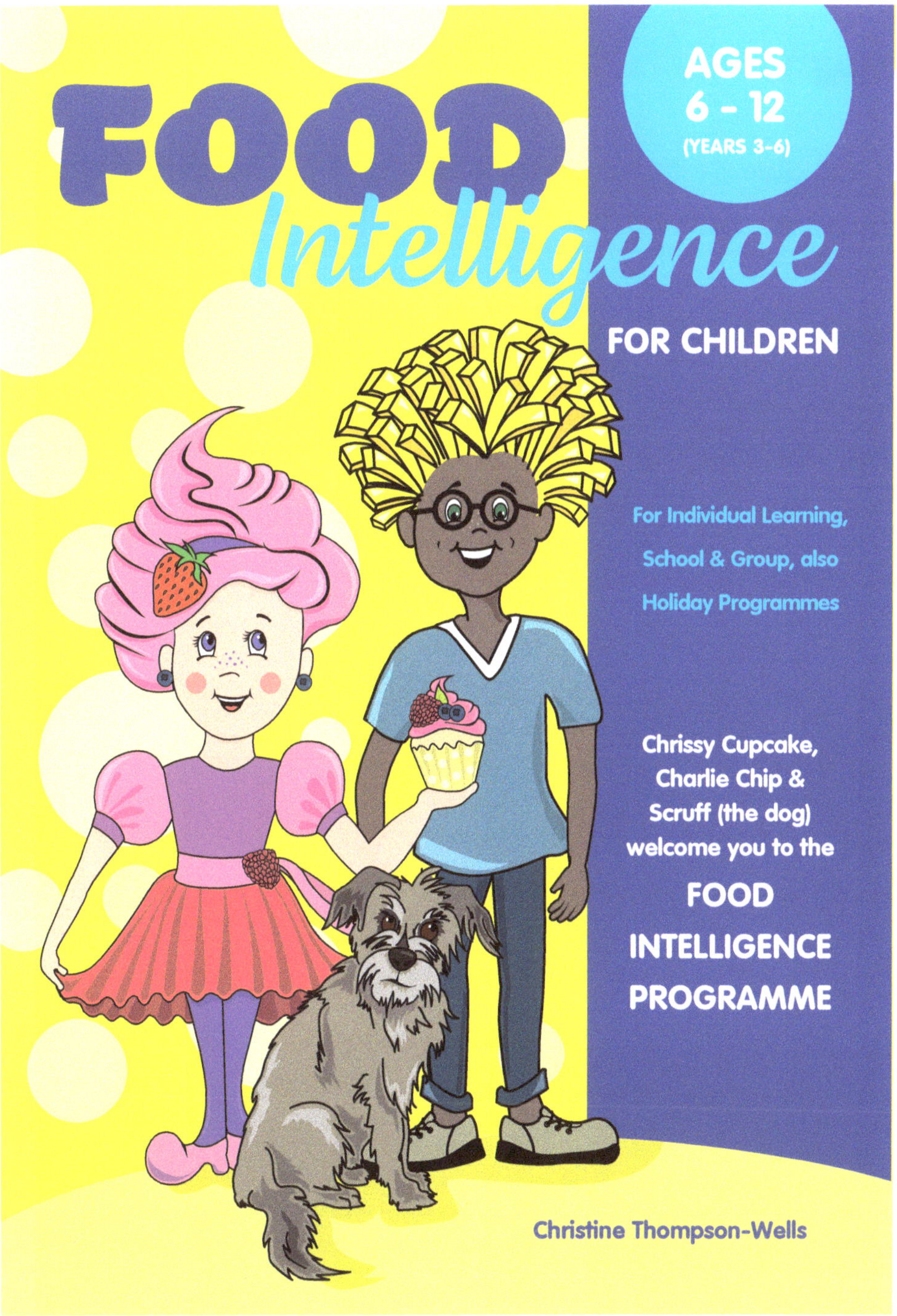

OBJECTIVE AND OUTCOME FOR THE CHILD

OBJECTIVE Meeting SCOOTLE (ACPPS058)

By the end of this short course, you will understand how to identify healthy food, which good food gives you energy, and which food to avoid. You will also understand the benefits of eating complex carbohydrate and the difference in eating empty carbohydrates.

OUTCOME

You will be able to make beneficial, good food choices that help your body to grow; you will have good energy to learn your lessons, play and have fun.

For teachers and programme providers, please see Meeting Curriculum Objectives, Nutrition Page 32.

If you have purchased this book without its cover, it may be a stolen book.
Neither the publisher or the author is under any obligation to provide professional services in anyway, legal, health or in any form which is related to this book, its contents advice or otherwise.

The law and practices vary from country to country and state to state. If legal or professional information is required, the purchaser, or the reader should seek the information privately and best suited to their particular needs, and circumstances.
The author and publisher specifically disclaim any liability that may be incurred from the information within this book.
All rights reserved.
No part of this book, including the interior design, images, cover design, diagrams, or any intellectual property (IP), icons and photographs may be reproduced or transmitted in any form by any means (electronic, photocopying, recording or otherwise) without the prior permission of the publisher. ©

Copyright© 2022 MSI Australia
All rights reserved.

Published by How2Books
Under licence from MSI Ltd, Australia
Company Registration No: 642923859
NSW, Australia
See our website: www.how2books.com.au
Or contact by email: admin@booksforreadingonline.com
Covers and Copyright owned by MSI, Australia

MSI acknowledges the author and images used in this book.

ISBN: 978-0-6451612-5-0

Working together

HEALTH WARNING

Some Children May Have Health Conditions Or Allergies To Some Of The Food Types Mentioned Today - Precautions Must Be In Place So That A Clear Understanding Of The Content Of The Presentation Is Understood.

Identifying You

Name..

Class Number or Name

....

Tell us about the food you like?
....
....
....

What is your favourite food?
1)...
2)..

What food don't you like?
....
....
....
....

YOUR WELLBEING & GOOD HEALTH

For you to grow, learn and play, you need to eat healthy food.

So why is it important to know about your food and where it comes from?

Understanding the origins of food and its importance to your health.

How important is it for you to eat healthy food?

Important............................

Not important....................

Don't know.....................?

Think for a moment...!
Why is it important to eat healthy food?

....

....

SO, HOW WOULD YOU DESCRIBE WHOLE, GOOD FOOD?

....
....
....
....

BEFORE WE START, YOU NEED TO KNOW ABOUT MOLECULES...!

So, what is a molecule?

INTRODUCING YOU TO GOOD AND BAD MOLECULES

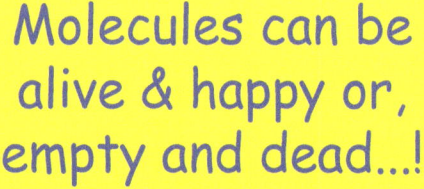

Molecule alive and happy - A Good Molecule

Molecule empty and dead - A Bad Molecule

Molecules can be alive & happy or, empty and dead...!

Molecules are in your food and in the air you breathe. As you know now, some molecules are alive and some are dead. The air you breathe in the country, has good molecules

THE IMPORTANCE OF EATING GOOD FOOD CONTAINING HEALTHY MOLECULES

To explain how many good molecules are in each bite of healthy food, let's take a banana, and cut that banana into 25mm pieces, it is estimated that there are 100,000,000 molecules in each piece...

Banana cube cut from fresh banana — 25mm

Because a molecule is so small, it cannot be seen with the naked eye!

Eating healthy food containing healthy molecules keeps your brain and body in good health. You have more energy to enjoy your play, learn your lessons and stay well.

Good food comes from healthy seas, soils, and rainfall

5 DIFFERENT FOOD TYPES

Within the food supply chain, there are 5 different foods listed that work with your body and brain to keep it healthy:

1) **Fruit and Vegetables** (Some of these are also known as Starchy foods)

   ....

2) Starchy foods including breads, pasta and rice

   ....

3) Dairy foods including milk, yogurt, cheese and cream

   ....

4) Protein including fish, meat and eggs

   ....

5) Healthy fats from some plants and nuts, lamb, goat and beef

   ....

GETTING TO KNOW YOUR FOOD

Discussing the food types

Fresh fruit and vegetables. Please think carefully, when was the last time you ate an apple?

....

....

Chrissy Cupcake in her slide has spoken of starchy foods, which include breads, pasta and rice. Who had some rice in their meal last night?

....

....

Dairy foods are important for your bones and body to grow, who has eaten some yogurt or cheese today?

....

....

Eating foods containing protein is important and protein allows your brain to grow and mature, who had fish, meat or eggs for tea or dinner on Friday?

....

....

Fat is important in all healthy diets, some of us don't like to eat fat because we think it is bad, who doesn't eat fat?

....

....

5 IMPORTANT FOODS FOR A HEALTHY DIET
GETTING TO KNOW YOUR FOOD - STARTING WITH FRUIT AND VEGETABLES AND IDENTIFYING THE MOLECULES

Fresh fruit and vegetables are important to eat because they provide you with good, sustainable energy. Who knows what sustainable means? It means long-term energy, all day energy. It also means after eating fresh or lightly cooked fruit or vegetables, you have a longer time to play, do your schoolwork or enjoy your holidays. Food that gives you this type of energy is called 'whole food' and is a complex carbohydrate. You will learn a lot about carbohydrates and complex carbohydrates as we go through our lessons. Many foods that are bought at fast-food take-away outlets have their good energy taken from them through processing.

Processing food allows it to be used in many different ways, and allows it to last longer on the supermarket or food-outlet shelves, this is not always a good idea.

Apples, carrots, parsnip, and fresh fruits are all good for you and once you eat them, your body works hard so that you feel good and healthy after eating them.

STARCHY FOODS
INCLUDING BREAD, PASTA AND RICE

Many foods contain starch. We have just spoken about apples on the previous page, they are not only a complex carbohydrate, but they are also a starchy fruit. Other foods that are starch and a complex carbohydrate is spaghetti, rice, bread, and bread rolls. Because these foods are complex carbohydrates, they are

satisfying to eat. If you eat too much of them, your tummy can feel uncomfortable after the meal. These foods also give you a lot of energy to play, have fun and enjoy your time.

When some of these foods are bought at fast-takeaway outlets or food chain stores, they are not always as healthy as they look. Sometimes, these foods have food additives added to make them look delicious to eat, but they are not always as good for you as they look.

Bread your adults buy at the baker's should be good to eat.

DAIRY FOODS
INCLUDING MILK, CHEESE AND YOGURT

Milk is used in many foods; it is good for your body, bones, and brain. When these foods come from cows, goat or lamb, your body feels happy, so you feel happy.

Many people like to eat yogurt, that is also very good for you. Natural yogurt does not have sugar added. We will talk about sugar a little later.

Many cheeses are made from cow and goat milk. Sheep milk is not so commonly used but is very good for you.

Natural cheese is another dairy food that is eaten worldwide and is a good food for building bones and teeth.

Do you like to drink milk? If so, you should only drink natural milk. If you want to flavour it, use natural or frozen berries or fresh fruit such as banana. It is good to drink a glass of natural milk every day.

PROTEIN FOOD
INCLUDING MEAT, FISH AND EGGS

When our diet includes protein, we are eating food that is good and allows us to learn new lessons, concepts, and work on our schoolwork. Protein also allows our muscles to grow so that we can take part in sport.

Eating freshly cooked fish and meat helps us to think clearly and to think things through.

Most meals contain some type of protein.

Eating eggs for breakfast are very good because they supply you with good energy and keep your tummy full. Sometimes, boiled eggs are served with fresh toast. Eggs are good to have in sandwiches, on toast, for picnics and going on long journeys; they are also good to have with salads and with many other foods.

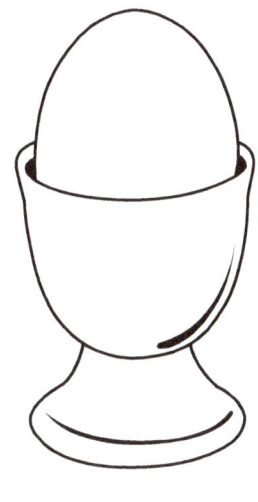
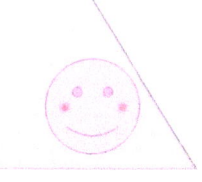

FATS INCLUDING PLANT AND ANIMAL FAT

Many foods we eat contain fat, just to mention a few: fish, meat, eggs, milk, cheese, yogurt, bread, some pasta when a meat sauce is added, or when butter or olive oil are added to different foods, fruit, and nuts.

Like all the other foods mentioned in this section, good foods, including good fat is important for the body and brain to remain healthy.

Avocados are a rich source of oil and contain many vitamins and minerals as well as their very good oil. Avocados, because of their natural health benefits, are now a very popular fruit.

Other foods that contain natural fat are, olives, peanuts, almonds, walnuts, cashew, and other nuts.

Good animal fat comes from goat, beef, and lamb.

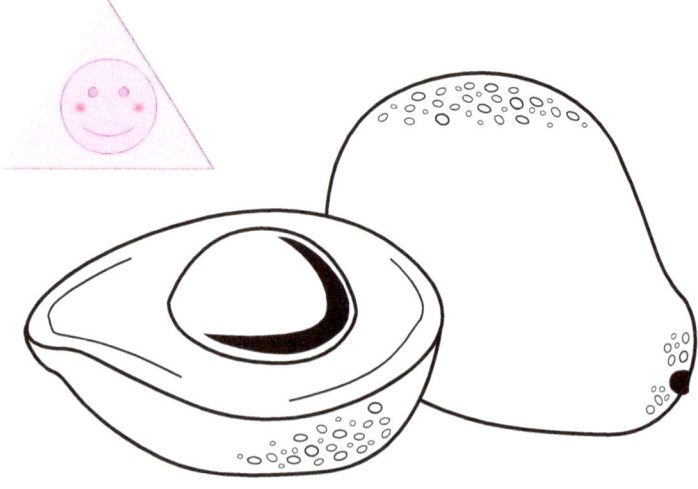

15

WHAT DO YOU NOW UNDERSTAND ABOUT THE 5 DIFFERENT TYPES OF FOOD YOU EAT?

Fruit and vegetables

....

....

Bread, pasta, and rice

....

....

Milk, cheese, and yogurt

....

....

Meat, Fish, and eggs

....

....

Fats, including plant and animal fats

....

....

YOUR NOTES

....

....

....

....

THE DIFFERENCE BETWEEN CARBOHYDRATES

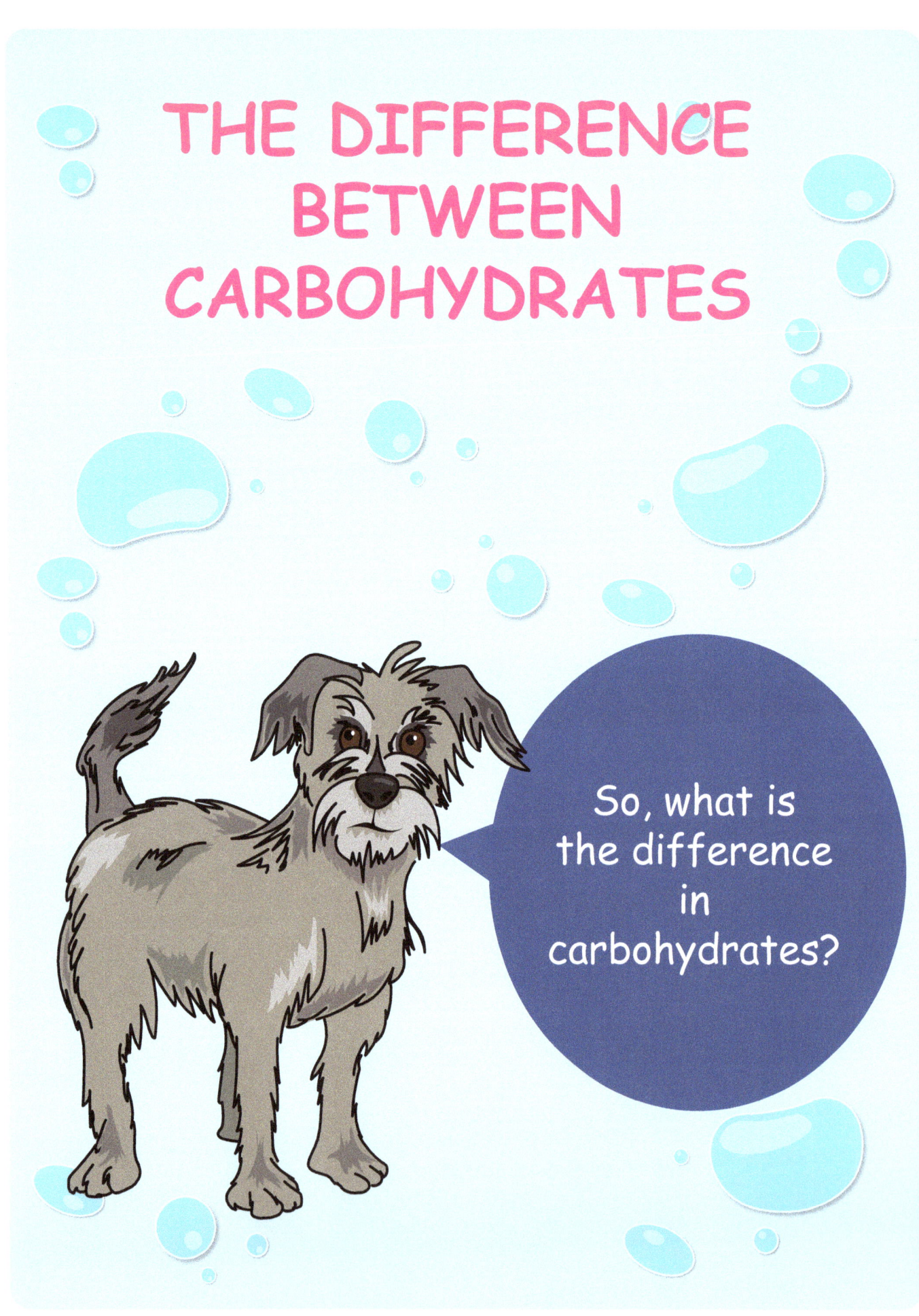

So, what is the difference in carbohydrates?

Most Good Foods Contain Complex Carbohydrates

BUT EMPTY CARBOHYDRATES ARE DIFFERENT

WHEN WE TALK ABOUT FOOD AND CARBOHYDRATES, WE NEED TO ASK: ARE THEY CARBOHYDRATES, OR ARE THEY COMPLEX CARBOHYDRATES?

Foods with complex carbohydrates are important in all diets. Complex carbohydrates are in good natural food; these complex carbohydrates give you the energy to learn your lessons, play, have fun and to enjoy your day.

When your food is missing in complex carbohydrates you feel tired, weak, unable to concentrate on your lessons and have fun when playing, this happens when you have eaten empty carbohydrate.

Your body and brain need complex carbohydrate, and not empty carbohydrate, so what is the difference between them?

> Your food can consist of complexed carbohydrates or empty carbohydrates, so what is the difference?

SO, WHY ARE COMPLEX CARBOHYDRATES SO GOOD FOR YOU?

Complex carbohydrates are found in food that is naturally grown in the ground. When your adults buy their greengrocery at the supermarket, from a farm or greengrocers; they possibly buy the food because they want

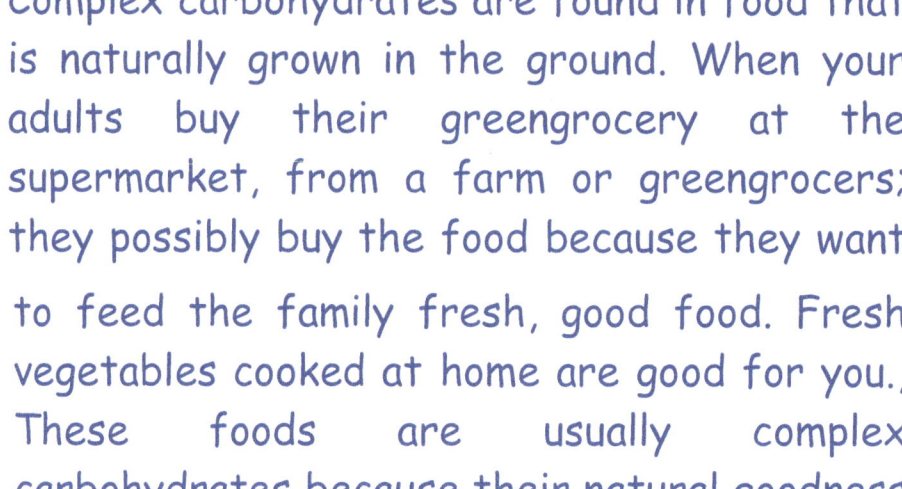

to feed the family fresh, good food. Fresh vegetables cooked at home are good for you., These foods are usually complex carbohydrates because their natural goodness is still in the vegetable, or fruit.

The foods that contain complex carbohydrate include some breads and bread rolls that are made from healthy flour without any sugar added. Other foods include fresh fruits, rice, pasta, and some nuts.

Sometimes we eat a combination of complex carbohydrates together. Sometimes your adults will cook many baked vegetables together which may include potatoes, pumpkin, or parsnips; these are all complex carbohydrate foods that give you lots of energy.

SO, WHY ARE EMPTY CARBOHYDRATES SO BAD FOR YOU?

Food made from sugar does not give to your body and brain any health benefit. Instead, sugary foods can add many health problems.

When you have eaten sugar, because of its processing, can also interfere with the way you feel, the way you play, with your friendships, and your schoolwork. You can find it difficult to, learn any new concepts or the way you listen to and work with your teacher and friends.

Once you have eaten sugary food, it will also make you want more sugary food…

Because you have become used to eating sugary food and as you grow up, your body and brain will want more sugary foods; your brain doesn't know the difference between a complex carbohydrate or an empty carbohydrate. Your brain only recognises the sweetness of sugar as you eat the empty carbohydrate.

Not only is empty sugar carbohydrate put into the food you eat but it is also put into many soft drinks you drink.

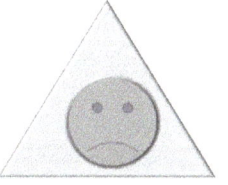

If that is so, why are empty carbohydrates different to complex carbohydrates?

A complex carbohydrate is packed with natural goodness. When an apple grows on the tree, it is watered by the rain that falls, and ripened by the sun that shines, that is why, it is so good for you to eat. This is true of all freshly grown food.

When you eat 'junk food' or 'processed food' that is made in a factory, the goodness of the food is lost and doesn't help your body or brain. Empty carbohydrates are in fast foods, bought at fast-food outlets, sweeties, lollies, some yogurt, cakes, biscuits, ice cream, and in foods containing processed sugar.

So complex carbohydrates are good to eat, and empty carbohydrate are bad to eat.

Please remember, sugar is an empty carbohydrate and gives no nutrition to your body or brain and can lead to you becoming sick.

If you love sweet foods, try eating natural honey on bread, in yogurt or ask an adult to add honey to their cake making instead of adding sugar.

YOU HAVE LEARNT A LOT ABOUT COMPLEX CARBOHYDRATES AND EMPTY CARBOHYDRATES

NOW, let's see if you can identify the following,

1) Is this bread complex carbohydrate [ ] or
an empty (dead) carbohydrate? [ ]

2) Are these frog cakes complex carbohydrate [ ] or empty (dead) carbohydrate? [ ]

3) Jacket potatoes are always a nice treat, are they a complex carbohydrate [ ] or an empty (dead) carbohydrate? [ ]

4) A doughnut with cream always looks good to eat, but is it a complex carbohydrate [ ] or an empty (dead) carbohydrate? [ ]

5) Jelly pineapples have a sugar coating, are they a complex carbohydrate [ ] or an empty (dead) carbohydrate? [ ]

ANSWERS 1) Complex, 2) Empty, 3) Complex, 4) Empty, 5) Empty.

SO WHAT IS PROTEIN?

We have previously spoken about proteins; proteins are large molecules that are found in fish, meat, and eggs, but protein does exist in other food like cheese, natural yogurt, nuts, and seeds.

Protein usually comes from animal-based foods which include cheese, milk, yogurt, and the foods we have already spoken about. The benefit of eating protein-based foods gives your body many building blocks that help to keep your body and brain healthy.

Protein-based foods help your immune system to stay healthy and quickly recover from illnesses.

Virus attacks like Covid, find it difficult to attack a healthy immune system. Protein-based foods also help in building strong bones and helps your body to work with the complex carbohydrates you eat; this gives you extra energy to play and learn.

 You can add thawed frozen fruit and honey to yogurt for a delicious snack after school. Yogurt will give you a lot of energy to do homework and the honey will keep your tastebuds zinging.

 All good protein will help you to build your muscles but fresh meat with other foods like mashed potatoes will, not only taste good, but help your body to grow, stay well and become stronger while you sleep at night.

 Nuts are a good source of protein and if you don't eat nuts, try eating peanut or almond butter with some slices of banana, it is delicious.

 Cheese is a good source of protein as are eggs and other protein-packed foods. All the foods containing protein also contain healthy molecules and this means, by eating them, your whole body and brain, will say, 'thank you.' And how does your body say, 'thank you?' You will know because you feel good, healthy and can enjoy doing the things you love to do.

WE NOW NEED TO ASK, WHAT ARE THE BENEFITS OF EATING GREEN FOODS?

THE BENEFITS OF EATING GREEN FOODS – GREEN AND LEAF VEGETABLES

There are many reasons to eat green and green leafy vegetables

1. They help your brain to work
2. They keep your stomach and gut happy
3. They help to keep your skin glowing and healthy
4. They help your bones to stay strong and healthy and this is essential if you want to play sport or be an athlete
5. As you get older, your body will stay healthier by eating green vegetables

6. If you should hurt yourself, the goodness in green leafy foods will help to fight infections

7. If you eat sugary foods in the future, by eating some green food, it will help to balance the sugar in your body's system

8. Because all of your eaten food needs to go through your body's system to digest it, green foods, will help with the digestion. Digesting your food properly, helps you to feel happy.

GREEN AND LEAF VEGETABLES

- HELPS YOUR BODY TO BUILD THE IRON IT NEEDS THAT KEEPS YOUR BLOOD HEALTHY
- GREEN FOODS HELP TO KEEP YOUR BRAIN HEALTHY
- THEY HELP TO KEEP YOUR SKIN HEALTHY AND LOOKING GOOD
- GREEN FOOD HELP YOUR BONES TO STAY STRONG
- THEY HELP YOUR GUT TO STAY HEALTHY AND SO YOU FEEL GOOD AND DON'T GET A TUMMY ACHE
- GREEN FOODS ALSO HELP TO BOOST YOUR IMMUNE SYSTEN AND WILL HELP TO KEEP YOU SAFE FROM VIRUSES LIKE COVID

GOING BACK TO THE FOOD YOU EAT

Now think back and try to think about the food you have eaten in your last meal and try to think of the following,

1. Did I have any green leaves or vegetables?
   [YES] [NO]
   If YES, what was it?
   ....

2. Did I eat any protein? [YES] [NO]
   If YES, what was it?
   ....

3. Did I eat any complex carbohydrate?
   If YES, what was it?
   ....

4. Did I eat any carbohydrate?
   If YES, what was it?
   ....

5. Did I eat an apple or a piece of fruit? If so, would you call that a complex carbohydrate?
   ....

YOUR NOTES

....

....

....

....

GOING BACK TO THE FOOD YOU EAT
The Journey of the Egg Sandwich

We all eat different foods in our meals, but in this story, we are going to focus on the journey of the egg sandwich. Once the egg sandwich is eaten, it goes on a long journey that helps to keep you feeling good and happy.

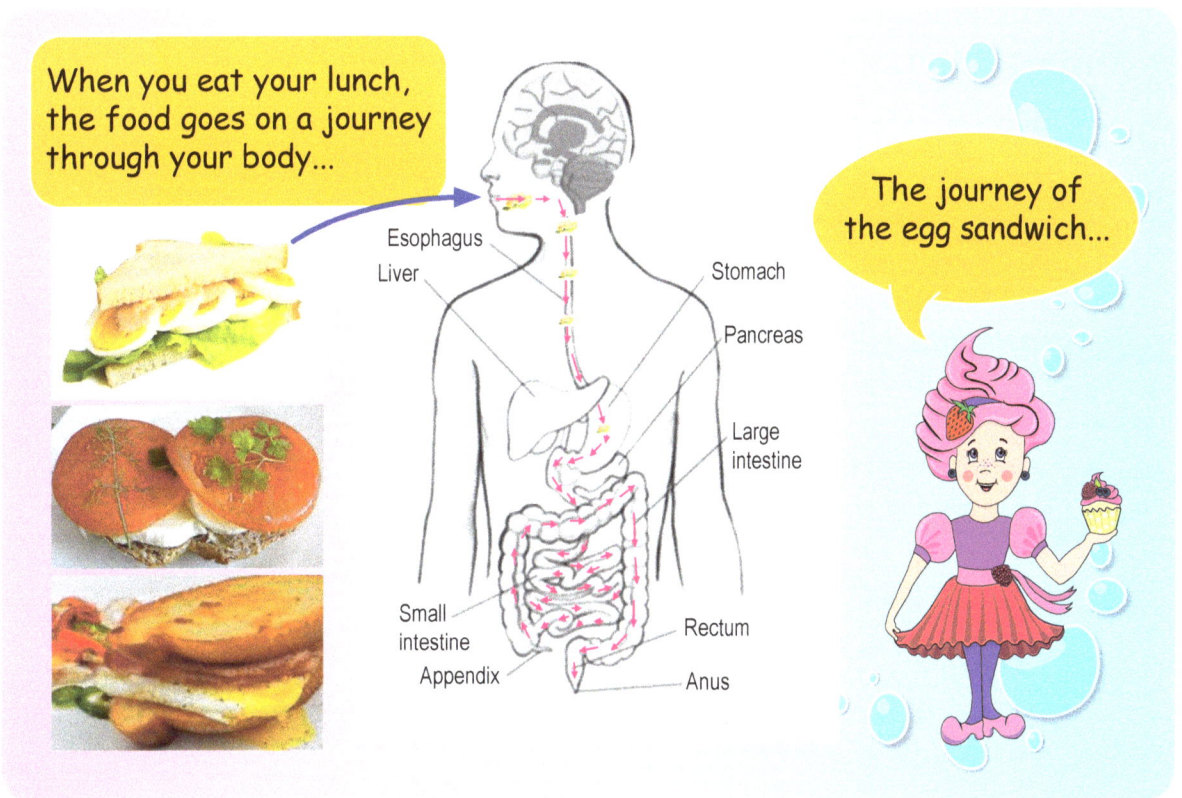

The journey of the egg sandwich,

1. First you need to eat the sandwich. You chew the food with your teeth before you swallow it and once this happens,
2. It passes from your mouth into your oesophagus; this is the long pipe shown with the red arrows in your workbook and on the slide. This chewed food then passes,
3. Into your stomach where the stomach acids will start to break down the content of the egg sandwich.

4. When this is done, it will pass to your small intestine. Please follow the red arrows in your workbook.
5. The intestine is a remarkable piece of body technology. It works by itself squeezing the egg sandwich which allows the vitamins and minerals to be released and these will then enter your blood giving you more energy.
6. From the small intestine, the left-over bits of the egg sandwich will go to your large intestine. Once the larger intestine has what it needs, it will pass the waste down through that intestine and then it will be released through the anus.

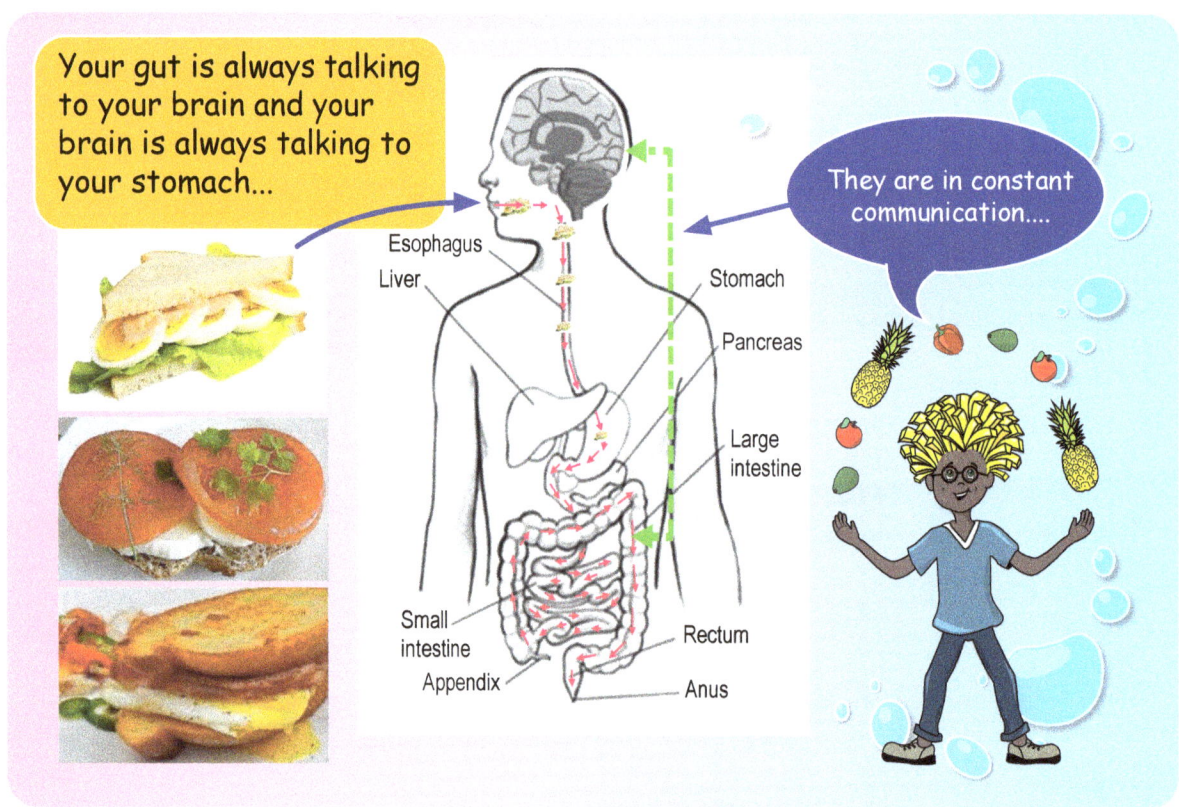

7. As the egg sandwich is digested between your stomach acid and gut, your brain and gut talk to each other. You don't know this is happening but your brain and gut work together, day and night sending each other messages about the goodness of the food you have eaten. If you have eaten bad food, then your gut will let your brain know and you will know by feeling sick.

During these two lessons, we have only covered part of the journey to Food Intelligence, there is still a long journey to go.

I hope you have enjoyed this programme of introduction to our Food Intelligence Programme, and we look forward to seeing you in Stage Two.

Christine

★ ★ ★ ★ ★

Congratulations

STAGE ONE

FOOD INTELLIGENCE

FOR CHILDREN 6 TO 11 YEARS

NAME……………………………………………………

DATE……………………………………………………

TEACHER………………………………………………

FOR TEACHERS AND PROGRAMME PROVIDERS

Meeting Curriculum Objectives
NUTRITION
SCOOTLE (ACPPS058)

FOOD INTELLIGENCE - FOR AUSTRALIA

Overview

The Australian Curriculum addresses learning about food and wellbeing in two ways:
- in content descriptions as in Health and Physical Education (HPE),
- Science and Technologies, noting that in HPE there is a food and nutrition focus area and in Design and Technologies there is a technologies context (food specialisations)

The scope of learning in food and wellbeing reflects relevant content from across the Australian Curriculum.

The Australian Curriculum Connection: Food and wellbeing provides a framework for all young Australians to understand and value the importance of good nutrition for health and wellbeing both across learning areas and specifically within the Technologies. Within the learning area as in the technology's context in the core learning across Foundation to Year 8 and as additional learning opportunities offered by states and territories in Years 9-10.

The food and wellbeing connection is presented in bands of schooling. In Foundation - Year 6, the connection is described as nutrition, health, and wellbeing. In Years 7-10, it is described as home economics.

Rationale

There are increasing community concerns about food issues, including the nutritional quality of food and the environmental impact of food manufacturing processes. Students need to understand the importance of a variety of foods, sound nutrition principles and food preparation skills when making food decisions to help better prepare them for their future lives. Students should progressively develop knowledge and understanding about the nature of food and food safety, and how to make informed and appropriate food preparation choices when experimenting with and preparing food in a sustainable manner.

The Design and Technologies food specialisations technologies context includes the application of nutrition principles (as described in Health and Physical Education) and knowledge about the characteristics and properties of food-to-food selection and preparation, and contemporary technology-related food issues.

When connecting the curriculum to plan a program of teaching and learning for nutrition, health, and wellbeing (F–6) or home economics (7–10), teachers draw on content from across the Australian Curriculum, in particular Health and Physical Education, and Design and Technologies.

Safety Consideration

In implementing projects with a focus on food, care must be taken, regarding food safety, and specific food allergies that may result in anaphylactic reactions. The Australasian Society of Clinical Immunology and Allergy has published guidelines for prevention of anaphylaxis in schools, preschools and childcare. Some states and territories have their own specific guidelines that should be followed. When state and territory curriculum authorities integrate the Australian Curriculum into local courses, they will include more specific advice on safety. For further information about relevant guidelines, contact your state or territory curriculum authority.

Dimensions

To maximise the effectiveness of any nutrition, health and wellbeing or home economics program delivered in schools, learning should be sequential. The dimensions of this learning are:

- individuals, families, and communities and
- nutrition and food specialisations.

ISBN: 978-0-6451612-5-0

www.ingramcontent.com/pod-product-compliance
Lightning Source LLC
Chambersburg PA
CBHW041712290426
44109CB00028B/2850